Topper Sailing

John Caig

Photographs by

Tim Hore

Fernhurst Books

© Fernhurst Books 1982 and 1987

First published 1982 by
Fernhurst Books
31 Church Road, Hove, East Sussex BN3 2FY

Revised edition published 1987

ISBN 0 906754 04 6

Acknowledgements

The publishers wish to thank Topper International
Ltd for supplying material for pages 4, 5 and
62-64, and the diagram on page 7.
    The photographs on page 4 were supplied by
Rolinx Ltd.
    Thanks are also due to Walton on Thames
Sailing Club, Island Barn Reservoir, East Molesey,
Surrey and to Queen Mary Sailing Club, Ashford,
Middlesex where the photographs were taken.
    The cover design is by Behram Kapadia and
the photograph is courtesy of Sepia Visual Arts.

Composition by Allset, London
Printed by Hollen Street Press, Slough
Printed and bound in Great Britain

FOREWORD

The Topper has a special place in the teaching of
sailing in Britain. Thousands of people learn the
basic skills of the sport in Toppers every year at
the hundreds of dinghy teaching establishments
recognised by the Royal Yachting Association. In
addition, no other class has done as much to in-
fluence the techniques of teaching beginners as
the Topper.
    It is not just a beginner's boat, as you will see
by reading the later chapters of this book. Topper
fleets are established at many sailing clubs, and
the class association organises a programme of
open meetings and championships for Topper
enthusiasts.
    Whether you are an absolute beginner or
already have the basic skills, you'll learn a great
deal by reading *Topper Sailing*. Better still, use
the book together with the RYA training video
At One with the Wind, which we have produced
specially for Topper sailors in conjunction with
Minorca Sailing Holidays and Topper
International.

    Good sailing!

John Driscoll
RYA National Sailing Coach

Contents

1 The Topper story

The Topper's astonishing success as the first truly mass-produced racing dinghy is the result of a series of chance meetings and the exceptional vision and dedication of a few enterprising men.

In the early 'seventies, John Dunhill was establishing a modest boat-building business and one day he chanced upon the moulds of a racy-looking little eleven-footer. Enquiries led him to the boat's designer, Ian Proctor, and he secured the right to build the boat — then named OD11 — in GRP (glass-reinforced plastic). John changed the name to Topper and the boat met with immediate success, coming out well on top in *Yachting World*'s 'one of a kind' dinghy rally in the summer of 1973.

At the London Boat Show, John Dunhill was approached by someone who told him that the company he represented — Rolinx Ltd, a subsidiary of ICI — had just developed a method of 'twinning' two enormous injection-moulding machines which would be capable of turning out Toppers in polypropylene at the rate of one every seven minutes; was he interested? Naturally he immediately responded to the long-term possibilities and, together with the directors of

Rolinx, set about the task of raising the necessary quarter of a million pounds to commission the injection-moulding tools. John had been most prudent in selling one of his GRP Toppers to a very senior executive in the Guinness Group and this man's enthusiasm for the boat — and later for the new production project — eventually led to Guinness taking over John Dunhill's company and providing 50 per cent of the initial tooling costs. The other half was put up by the National Research Development Corporation who clearly felt that the project was not only viable but of great importance to the prestige of Britain's world-leading plastics technology.

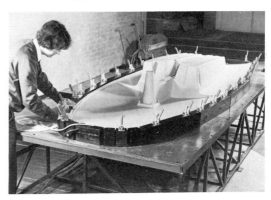

Copper braid is being inserted around the gunwale line of the deck moulding. The hull moulding is then clamped tightly on top. When electric current is passed through the braid, the two parts are permanently fused together.

In 1977 the Topper received the Design Council award and Topper International Ltd (formerly J. V. Dunhill Boats Ltd) has now sold over 29,000 Toppers worldwide. Boats have been exported to over thirty countries and the dinghy has introduced thousands of people to an inexpensive but exciting new sport.

The Topper is built from two injection mouldings — one for the hull and one for the deck. This is a hull moulding lying alongside half of the die which was used to make it.

2 Car Toppering

The Topper got its name in the first place because of the ease with which it could be transported on the roof of a car and this great mobility has certainly played a considerable part in the boat's worldwide success. The inverted boat presents a smooth, aerodynamic shape to the wind and neither speed nor fuel consumption are greatly affected during 'car toppering'. In fact, many caravan owners claim an improvement in consumption when towing because the Topper's shape guides the airflow around the bluff front of their 'vans. In spite of the simplicity of the operation there are some important guidelines to follow if — like me — you drive many thousands of miles each year beneath a Topper.

Position the two roof bars as far apart as possible on the car roof up to about a 4-foot maximum. It is quite acceptable for them to be much closer together than this as may be necessary if you drive a coupe or rigid-topped sports car. Load the Topper upside down, bow forward and ensure that the front bar supports the side decks immediately behind the aft end of the foredeck. Ideally, the rear bar should support the side deck immediately ahead of the stern deck. Quick-release straps are by far the simplest means of securing the Topper and the least likely to come undone. If the bars are wide enough, you can lay the spars alongside the hull and take the straps right around the whole lot, which will greatly reduce loading time. *Always* tie the boat down to the bumpers (fenders) fore and aft. The bow painter can be used forward — this will stop the wind from lifting the boat — and the horse can be used aft, where it will check any tendency for the boat to run forward in an emergency stop. If you are using a beach trolley, this can be carried on the upside-down hull.

It is quite feasible to carry two Toppers on the roof of most cars but remember that the all-up weight will be 190 lb. The lower hull should be loaded *right way up*, bow pointing aft with the rear roof bar under the mast position. The upper hull should be loaded upside down, bows forward. You will find that two Toppers fit together very snugly in this way — but do make sure that they are very well strapped down.

3 Parts and rigging

The Topper is exceptionally simple and is supplied complete and ready to sail. The diagram opposite shows all the standard parts in place. A few modifications are shown on pages 45-47; you may find these helpful if you want to race.

Rudder/tiller assembly

It is a good idea to check the tightness of both the nut and bolt holding the tiller to the rudder and the similar nut and bolt connecting the rudder to its stock. To give positive steering you should avoid any slack in these areas. Also, if the tiller bolt is loose you may find that you lift the rudder by mistake when tacking.

You may be surprised to discover that the daggerboard floats. However the rudder assembly — due to its cast alloy stock — does not! Be careful therefore when shipping or unshipping the rudder when afloat.

Toestraps

The length of the toestraps is not adjustable but to help you get your feet under them quickly, tie the two towards each other as tightly as possible with the black line provided. Do this either just behind the daggerboard case or near the aft end of the cockpit. Personally I favour the latter position for this tie since it gives more freedom of movement at the forward end of the cockpit.

Burgee (flag)

Many people like to use a racing flag (square) or burgee (triangular) to give them a constant reminder of the wind direction. The mast top of the Topper is designed for the optional flag to be pushed in and retained by an internal clip. An alternative is to wind tape around the stem of the flag and push it through the hole in the bow of the boat. I find this extremely useful, particularly on the run.

SAIL CONTROLS

In addition to the primary sail control — the mainsheet — the other three controls affecting the shape of the mainsail are the outhaul, the downhaul and the kicking strap (vang). Each controls the amount or position of the curve (belly) in the sail which should be adjusted to suit different wind conditions, as explained later. For your first sail, tension the controls as follows.

Outhaul

This should be tensioned initially to give a slight curve in the foot of the sail. The maximum draft should not exceed three to four inches between sail and boom at the midpoint.

Downhaul

Tension this so it just removes any creases in the leading edge of the sail when the mainsheet is pulled tight.

Kicking strap or vang

The 'normal' tension for this is achieved by first tensioning the mainsheet and then taking up the slack on the kicking strap line so it is just tight. This will give the correct tension on the boom when reaching or running. Since the mainsheet will be varied in tension for different wind conditions the kicking strap should be varied accordingly. It is not easy to adjust the kicking strap while actually reaching or running except in very light winds.

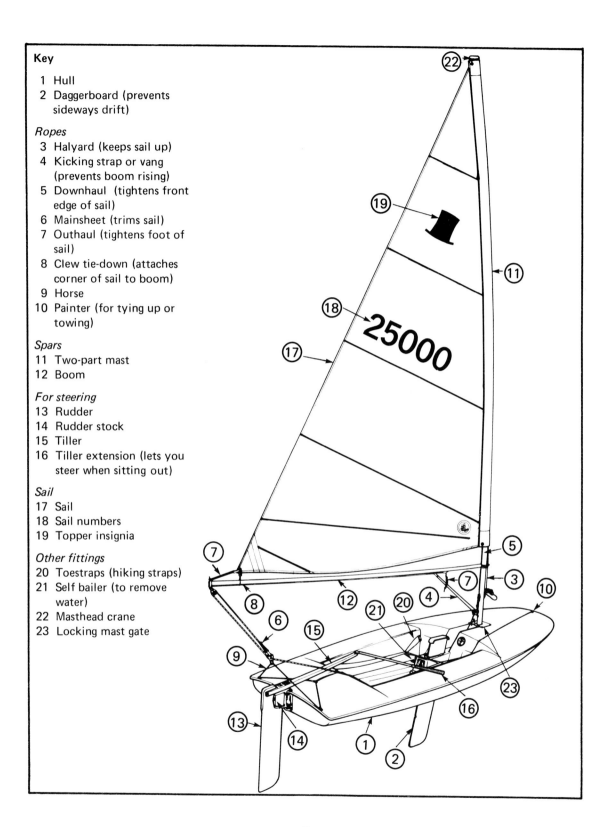

Key

1 Hull
2 Daggerboard (prevents sideways drift)

Ropes
3 Halyard (keeps sail up)
4 Kicking strap or vang (prevents boom rising)
5 Downhaul (tightens front edge of sail)
6 Mainsheet (trims sail)
7 Outhaul (tightens foot of sail)
8 Clew tie-down (attaches corner of sail to boom)
9 Horse
10 Painter (for tying up or towing)

Spars
11 Two-part mast
12 Boom

For steering
13 Rudder
14 Rudder stock
15 Tiller
16 Tiller extension (lets you steer when sitting out)

Sail
17 Sail
18 Sail numbers
19 Topper insignia

Other fittings
20 Toestraps (hiking straps)
21 Self bailer (to remove water)
22 Masthead crane
23 Locking mast gate

25000

1 Set up the horse as shown. Shackle on the mainsheet block. Shackle the other mainsheet block to the boom. Tie a knot in the free end of the mainsheet.

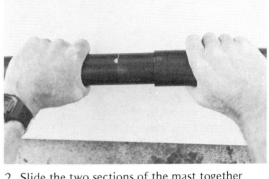

2 Slide the two sections of the mast together making sure the red dots are aligned.

5 Go back to the foot of the mast, pull the halyard very tight and make fast to the cleat at the front of the mast.

6 Point the boat into the wind. Support the mast at an angle and engage the base of the mast in the cup under the mast gate.

9 Clip the downhaul through both cringles (holes) in the sail and make fast to the cleat at the back of the mast. Fit the rowlock end of the boom (gooseneck) onto the mast immediately above the collar. Either lead the downhaul outside the rowlock or pass it through the hole in the rowlock.

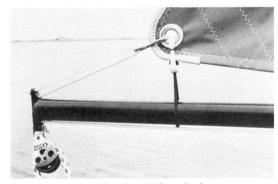

10 Set up the outhaul and clew tie-down as shown. Pull the outhaul fairly tight and cleat near the other end of the boom.

3 Make a loop in one end of the halyard. Pass the other end through the crane, and cleat tightly near the mast foot. This will hold the mast together while you thread it through the sail.

4 When the mast appears through the top of the sail, undo the loop and tie the halyard to the top of the sail. If you're using a flag, fit it into the top of the mast.

7 Pull the cord to close the gate and push in the toggle firmly.

8 Tie a safety knot in the toggle rope.

11 Attach the kicking strap as shown.

12 Arrange the rudder in the 'up' position. Pass the tiller under the rope horse and attach the rudder to its fittings (pintles). The blade is lowered by lifting and pushing back on the tiller.

4 Sailing theory

Take a careful look at this photograph. You will see that:

- The helmsman sits on the windward side of the boat (to balance the wind pushing on the sail).

- The helmsman always holds the tiller in his aft (back) hand. He steers with the tiller.

- The helmsman always holds the mainsheet in his forward (front) hand. The mainsheet adjusts the angle of the sail to the centreline of the boat.

How does the boat sail?

Wind is the Topper's driving force. The wind flows over the windward side of the sail (causing pressure) and round the leeward side (causing suction). The resulting force on the sail is in the direction of arrow A, i.e. it is at right angles to the sail.

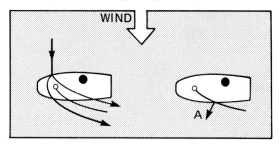

The force pushes the boat forwards and sideways. The forwards push is welcome! The sideways push is counteracted by water pressure on the daggerboard.

The helmsman's weight counteracts the heeling (capsizing) effect. The further he leans out, the more leverage he gets.

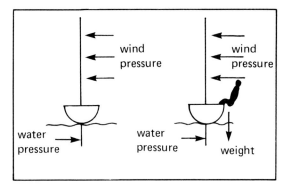

If the sail is pulled in, force A will be almost at right angles to the boat: the sideways force is maximum, and the daggerboard needs to be

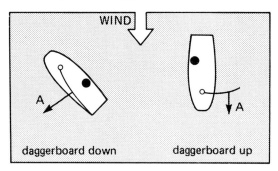

daggerboard down   daggerboard up

pushed right down to counteract it. If the sail is let out, force A points forwards: there is no sideways force, so the daggerboard can be pulled up.

How can I steer?

When a boat is sailing straight, the water flows past the rudder undisturbed. When the rudder is turned, the water is deflected. The water hitting the rudder pushes it, and the back of the boat, in direction B. The bow turns to the left.

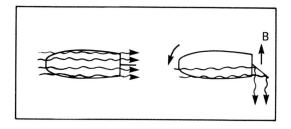

In short, pulling the tiller towards you turns the bow away from you, and vice versa.

How can I stop?

It is the wind in the sail that makes a boat go forward. To stop it, take the wind out of the sail either by letting go of the mainsheet, or by altering course towards the wind.

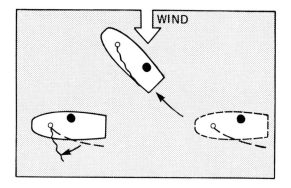

How can I tell which way the wind is blowing?

Everything in sailing is related to the wind direction. You can tell which way it's blowing by the feel of it on your cheek, by the wave direction or by using a burgee. Remember the burgee points to where the wind is going.

POINTS OF SAILING

Look at Figure 5 on the opposite page. There are three points of sailing:

1 *Reaching*—the boat sails *across* the wind (see Figure 1).
2 *Beating*—the boat sails *towards* the wind (Figure 2).
3 *Running*—the boat sails with the wind *behind* (Figure 3).

Reaching

The boat in Figure 1 is reaching. It is sailing at right angles to the wind, which is blowing from behind the helmsman's back. The sail is about halfway out and the daggerboard halfway up.

Beating

If you want to change course towards the wind, you must push the daggerboard down and pull in the sail as you turn. You can go on turning towards the wind until the sail is pulled right in. Then you are *beating* (Figure 2).

If you try to turn further towards the wind, you enter the 'no go area'. The sail flaps and the boat stops.

To get from A to B, the only way is to *beat* in a zigzag fashion (Figure 4).

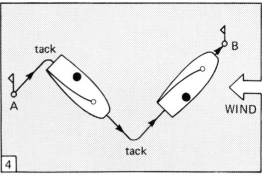

At the end of each 'zig' the boat turns through an angle of 90°. This is called a *tack*. The boat turns 'through' the wind — the sail blows across to the other side and the helmsman must shift his weight across the boat to balance it.

Running

From a reach, you may want to change course away from the wind. Pull up the daggerboard (not more than three-quarters up) and let out the sail as you turn. You can go on turning until the wind is coming from behind the boat. Then you are *running* (Figure 3).

If you turn more, the boat will *gybe*. The wind blows from the other side of the sail, which flicks across to the other side of the boat. You must shift your weight across to balance it.

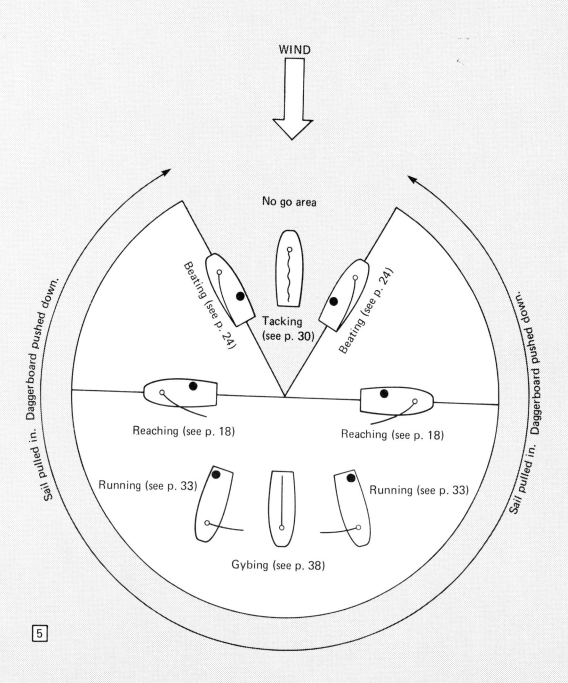

WIND

No go area

Beating (see p. 24)

Tacking
(see p. 30)

Beating (see p. 24)

Sail pulled in. Daggerboard pushed down.

Sail pulled in. Daggerboard pushed down.

Reaching (see p. 18)

Reaching (see p. 18)

Running (see p. 33)

Running (see p. 33)

Gybing (see p. 38)

5

5 A first sail

A dry run ashore

Before setting sail for the first time it is a very good idea to rig the boat completely, place it on a soft surface such as grass, and practise steering (with the rudder and daggerboard up, of course!), adjusting the mainsheet, tacking, etc. This will give you much more confidence when you finally go afloat.

First time afloat

Try to choose a day with a gentle breeze for your first sail. Wind is measured either on the Beaufort scale or in knots. Force 4 (11 knots) or above would be unsuitable.

A reservoir, river or estuary is a good place to learn to sail. If you are learning on the open sea, try to avoid an offshore wind (wind blowing from shore to sea) — you may get blown a long way from the shore. Always wear a lifejacket, and stay with the boat whatever happens.

Rig the boat as described in Chapter 3. Reef (page 16) if there's much wind. Get a friend to help you launch (page 17); he should hold the boat for you while you lower the rudder and put in the daggerboard — then one good push and you're under way.

As soon as you can, get sailing on a reach (Fig. 1) with the wind blowing at right angles to the boat. The daggerboard should be about half up and the sail about half out. Sit on the side opposite the sail. Practise adjusting the mainsheet and steering. Try to get the 'feel' of the boat, particularly using your weight to balance the wind in the sail. (Reaching is discussed in Chapter 8.)

Eventually you will need to tack (turn round — Figure 2) and reach back again. Tacking is described on pages 30-31. Try to tack smoothly, changing sides and swapping hands on the tiller and mainsheet as you do so. If the boat stops during a tack, keep the tiller central and wait until the boat starts to drift backwards. Eventually it will turn to one side and you'll be able to get sailing again.

Reach back and forth until you feel confident. Try picking an object and sailing straight towards it, adjusting the mainsheet so the sail is as far out as possible without flapping. If a gust comes, let the mainsheet out (Figure 3). Try to keep the boat moving.

Next try picking objects slightly closer to or slightly further away from the wind. Try sailing towards them, adjusting the mainsheet.

When you have had enough, head for the shore taking care to pull up the daggerboard and rudder in good time. Just before stepping out of the boat ease the sheet right out and head into the wind — making sure the water is shallow! Landing is discussed in more detail in Chapter 14.

Sailing two up

Although the class rules, at the time of writing, do not permit more than one person in the boat when racing, two people can have great fun in a Topper (Figure 4).

To stop the stern dragging in the water and slowing the boat down, it is important that both helm and crew sit as far forward as possible. This also helps when tacking — so long as the crew at the front is careful to duck under the kicking strap when crossing the boat. When running or reaching in light winds, the boat is easily balanced by one person sitting on each side deck.

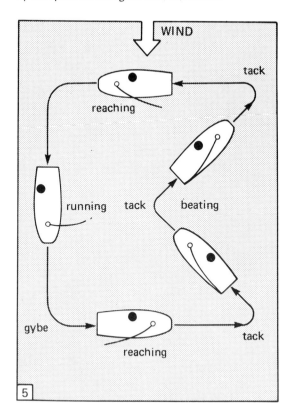

The next steps

When you feel happy reaching and tacking, you are ready to try the other points of sailing (see page 12). You should still reef if there is much wind (more than force 2).

One good way to practise is to sail round a square 'course' (Figure 5).

From your reach, gradually turn away from the wind, letting out the sail and pulling the daggerboard three-quarters up. You are now running. After a while, pull the tiller towards you, and gybe. Now reach the other way, with the daggerboard half down and the mainsheet half out. Next, push the daggerboard right down and turn towards the wind pulling in your sail. You are beating. Tack, and beat the other way. When you are far enough into the wind, turn off on to a reach, letting the sail out and pulling the daggerboard half up. Try several laps.

Remember:

- Sit on the windward side.

- Keep the mainsheet in your front hand, tiller in your back hand.

- If you get out of control, let go of the mainsheet.

6 Reefing

You need to reef (reduce sail) when the wind is strong. If you think you will have difficulty in holding the boat up on the beat, or will capsize on the run, then reef.

The Topper has been carefully designed so that you can reef out at sea. However, for the first few times you will find it easier to work on land or at the jetty. Here are the steps you take.

1 Start with the sail rigged normally. Re-rig the halyard, passing it through the eye in the sail. Unclip and 'tidy' the downhaul and kicking strap (vang).

2 Ease out the outhaul. Rotate the mast making sure the halyard moves properly inside the gooseneck. Continue until the sail has three rolls.

3 Tighten the outhaul and re-rig the kicking strap (vang). You do not use the downhaul when reefed. This photo shows a typical reduction in sail area.

4 If the wind drops, take out the reefs: point the boat into the wind, unclip the kicking strap, unroll the sail and tighten the outhaul. Re-rig the kicking strap and downhaul, pull in the mainsheet and you're away again.

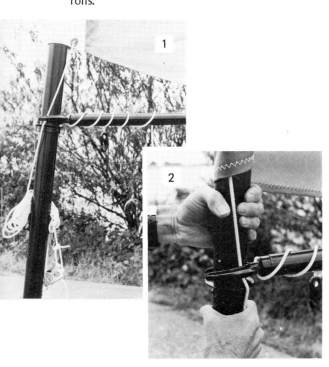

7 Launching

Always rig the boat before launching; if you are sailing from a jetty the sail can be rolled up completely around the mast and unfurled just before you set off.

Put the rudder on but pull it right up. Launch the boat on its trolley (if you have one), keeping it pointing into the wind all the time. Once the boat is floating you can slide the trolley out and pass it to a friend.

Always use the trolley to launch and retrieve your Topper — without it you are very likely to scratch the bottom of the boat.

Launching from a beach with an offshore wind

This is the easiest wind direction to launch in (Figure 1). Turn the boat slightly away from the wind, jump in, push a little rudder and daggerboard down. Pull in the mainsheet slightly and sail slowly into deeper water (direction A), where you can put the rudder and board right down. Don't try to sail hard or allow the boat to heel excessively with the rudder up or you may damage the rudder fastenings.

Launching with an onshore wind

This is more difficult since you will need to beat in shallow water to get away from the shore. Launch with the rudder up and the boat pointing into the wind. Choose the tack which takes you away from the shore at the greatest angle; push off, getting as much daggerboard down as the depth will allow as early as possible (Figures 2-4).

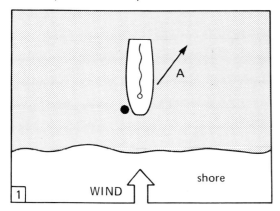

8 Reaching

Reaching is the easiest point of sailing and in a breeze the fastest and most exciting.

What is reaching?

The Toppers in Figure 1 are reaching. Their courses are roughly at right angles to the wind.

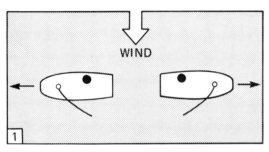

Adjusting the sail

The secret of reaching is sail trim. Always try to let the sail out as far as it will go without flapping.

Although the wind may vary in direction from moment to moment it is always possible when reaching to continue to steer in the direction that you wish to go. However, to maintain the fastest speed you must continually adjust the position of the boom, and hence the sail, via the mainsheet. Every few seconds, ease the mainsheet out until the front edge of the sail (luff) begins to lift and then pull it in until this flapping ceases (Figure 2).

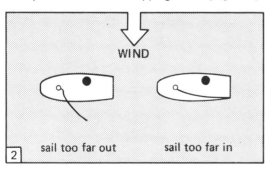

sail too far out   sail too far in

When you alter course you will have to adjust the sail angle accordingly. As you luff up (point your boat nearer the wind direction) pull the sail in, and as you bear away (point your boat away from the wind direction) ease the sail out.

Steering

Try to keep a reasonably straight course. Everything being equal the shortest distance between two points is a straight line! Remember every time you move the rudder you slow the boat very slightly.

Trim

The trim of the boat (the angle at which the hull sits in the water) is affected by the wind strength, the boat's speed and, above all, the location of your body weight. Sit forward in light winds to reduce the amount of hull skin in the water (and so reduce skin friction). Move aft in strong winds to lift the bow and help the boat skim over the water – this is planing. Do not allow the boat to heel excessively since this will encourage the boat to turn into the wind. You will have to take corrective action with the rudder (with associated braking) to maintain a straight course – this is called 'weather helm'.

Bear away each time a wave picks up the boat and try to surf on the wave.

Daggerboard

The daggerboard should not be fully down when reaching. The less you have down the less will be the drag resistance, and therefore the faster you will go. Half board is a good starting point, more being needed as you luff closer to the wind to stop you slipping sideways.

Sail controls

The sail should be set with a good curve or belly in it. The kicking strap (vang) should be normal but the outhaul and downhaul should both be eased considerably. At least 4 inches between the foot of the sail and the boom at its midpoint is desirable.

Gusts

When overpowered (i.e. when the wind is too strong for you to hold the boat flat without letting the sail flap) ease the mainsheet and bear away from the wind. Sheet in again and luff back to your normal course only when the gust has passed.

Going faster

Fast reaching helps win races. Here are some important points.

- Adjust the mainsheet continually.

- Keep the boat upright all the time. Sit out hard rather than ease the mainsheet to spill wind. Move back in the gusts and forward again as the wind drops.

- Steer a straight course (except during gusts).

- Look over your shoulder to see if a gust is coming — the water looks darker where a gust is travelling across it. When the gust hits bear away and sit out harder and ease the mainsheet a little. As the gust passes, luff up, sit inboard and pull the mainsheet in again.

The photo below shows good reaching style. The helmsman is using his weight to keep the boat absolutely level. His attention is on the front part of the sail (as well as where he's going!) and he continually adjusts the mainsheet. Because the boat is level, he can steer gently and easily. The kicking strap (vang) is tight, but the other controls are loose. The sail has a good curve in it for maximum power.

REACHING IN LIGHT WINDS

Reaching in light winds, like all light wind sailing, needs patience. Keep very still so as not to shake the shape out of the sail. If you need to move, do so slowly.

Trim

Sit forward to lift the stern out of the water and reduce the wetted area of the hull, and hence skin friction.

Heel the boat to windward if there is sufficient wind to fill the sail, holding the boom out with your forward hand. This reduces the wetted area still further and neutralises the weather helm normally created by the sail effort turning the boat into the wind.

In extremely light airs sit to leeward on the foredeck just behind the mast. This reduces the wetted area to a minimum and helps hold some shape in the sail.

Gusts

When a puff arrives, bear away to try and stay with it as long as possible. Above all this will take you below the direct line to the next mark and enable you to luff up in the lulls, thereby increasing your speed by up to 50 per cent in certain conditions.

Sail controls

The downhaul and outhaul should be loose. The kicking strap (vang) should be slightly looser than normal. Aim for a lot of curve in the sail (see photo below).

Steering

Move the tiller as infrequently and slowly as possible.

REACHING IN STRONG WINDS

Reaching in a Topper is extremely exhilarating in a blow. You are close to the water so the sensation of speed is remarkable.

Trim

Sit back enough to bring the bow up and promote a good planing angle. In *very* strong winds hike from the middle of the side deck (this is the widest part of the boat so your weight gives the maximum righting effect here).

Gusts

When overpowered (i.e. when the wind is too strong for you to hold the boat flat without letting the sail flap) bear away from the wind, luffing back above the direct course only when the gust passes. Never let the sail flap more than is necessary to keep the boat flat and always sit out as far as possible. In this way you will keep the maximum power full on.

Sail controls

In strong winds the kicking strap (vang), outhaul and downhaul should be set up quite tightly and not touched (in any case you would find it difficult to make adjustments in these conditions).

Daggerboard

With the daggerboard half up (the elastic retainer in the third notch) there will be adequate board in the water to offset the sideways forces, yet not enough to create excessive drag.

REACHING — SOME COMMON MISTAKES

1 This boat is heeling too much. Note the way the helmsman is having to pull the tiller to keep the boat on course. He should sit out further.

2 Here the downhaul and outhaul have been pulled too tight — note the creases along the front and bottom edges of the sail.

3 This helmsman is allowing the front edge of the sail to flap. He should pull in the mainsheet until the sail *just* stops flapping.

4 The effect of a loose kicking strap (vang) is to let the boom rise too high. The sail loses power, and the boat may capsize to windward in a gust.

9 Beating

Beating to windward in a Topper is particularly satisfying. The boat is so lively and responsive that it's a joy to sail in virtually all conditions.

What is beating?

A boat cannot sail straight from A to B (Figure 1). The sail will flap, and the boat will be blown backwards. The only way is to beat — to sail a zigzag course at an angle of about 45° to the wind.

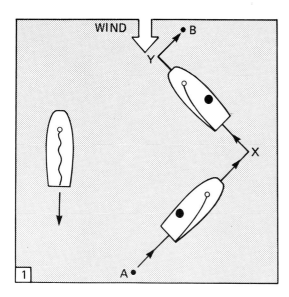

Steering

To beat, pull in the mainsheet until the mainsheet block and boom end block *nearly* touch; sit out, and steer as close to the wind as you can. The course is a compromise: if you steer too close to the wind you slow down, even though you are pointing closer to B. If you steer too far from the wind, you go faster, but are pointing well away from B (Figure 2).

The simplest check on your course is to watch the front of the sail. Turn towards the wind until the sail begins to flap, then turn back until it just stops flapping. You are now on course. Repeat this every few seconds — both to check your course, and because the wind constantly changes its direction.

At points X and Y the boat tacks through about 90°. Tacking is discussed on page 30.

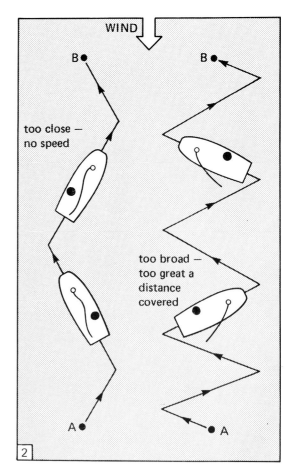

Adjusting the horse

Normally the horse should be pulled in tight — very tight in strong winds and only eased very slightly in light winds.

Adjusting the sail

When beating in medium or light winds there is no need to adjust the mainsheet. Keep it pulled in, and concentrate on using the tiller to keep the boat at the proper angle to the wind.

The tension on the mainsheet is important. In medium winds, pull it in until the mainsheet and boom end blocks are nearly touching. In light and in very strong winds, you will need to let the mainsheet out a little.

Trim

Sit forward, right up against the bulkhead, then either sit out or slide down to leeward with knees bent depending on the wind strength — you should aim for a constant 10° heel to reduce skin friction. Don't allow the boat to heel further than this in strong winds.

Daggerboard

The daggerboard should be right down when beating.

Gusts

You should learn to spot a gust approaching by the dark pattern (tiny wavelets) that it creates on the water. As it arrives luff up slightly and sit out hard — it is much easier to prevent the boat from heeling than to recover when it does!

Windshifts

The wind constantly alters in direction. However, some changes are larger and/or last longer. These are windshifts, and it is vital you spot them and react to them when racing. Windshifts are discussed on page 57.

Sail controls

The sail should be flattened off when beating to reduce heeling forces and drag. The stronger the wind the flatter it needs to be.

The *downhaul* (Cunningham) should be set just to remove the horizontal creases in light winds, and tightened progressively as the wind gets stronger. This tension affects the whole of the sail and pulls the draft (maximum curve) of the sail forward, reducing drag.

The *outhaul* should normally be set to give 4 inches of draft in the middle of the foot in light and medium winds. It needs to be tensioned as the wind increases until it is curling the foot upwards in overpowering conditions. This control affects the draft in the lower part of the sail only.

The *kicking strap* (vang) is more effective with the newer 1½-inch diameter boom which is rather less flexible than the original 1¼-inch version.

In certain conditions such as beating in heavy weather or sailing in a choppy sea the mast bend can be retained with the kicking strap while the mainsheet (and boom) is eased out to reduce the hook-back of the leech.

Kicking strap tension is quite critical when reaching. It needs to be slightly less tight when sailing over waves in light weather but quite tight in smooth water, particularly in strong winds (i.e. tighter than just taking up the slack after the mainsheet is pulled block to block).

Going faster

Fast beating is essential for racing since the majority of races start on a beat. Here are some points to watch and ideas to try:

- Never allow the boat to heel excessively.

- Sit out hard in strong winds. Only ease the mainsheet as a last resort.

- Keep the mainsheet pulled in tight except in light or very strong winds.

- Watch the front of the sail like a hawk. Keep trying to luff up, yet bear away every time the sail starts to flap.

- Keep a good look-out for other boats.

- Watch for windshifts.

BEATING IN LIGHT WINDS

Patience and stealth are the order of the day. Move around the boat as little as possible; when you must, move slowly taking care not to shake the shape out of the sail.

Setting the horse and mainsheet

Ease the horse about 2 inches. With the mainsheet now eased a little the boom will still stay approximately over the corner of the transom. Always remember that maximum speed through the water is more important than good pointing in these conditions since a well sailed boat can quite easily go twice as fast as a badly sailed one.

Steering

Continually watch the luff of the sail, bearing away immediately if it begins to lift. It is permissible to raise the rudder by one notch to increase the weather helm in these conditions and give more responsive steering.

Trim

Sit over the well between the daggerboard and the leeward deck with your knees bent double and your legs along the leeward side deck. This heels the boat which helps fill the sail (by gravity) and reduce hull-to-water skin friction. Heel the boat until the leeward gunwale is nearly under water.

Sail controls

The *downhaul* (Cunningham) should be loose — barely removing the creases from the sail.

The *outhaul* should be normal (i.e. 4 inches of draft in the middle of the foot) and tightened slightly in *extremely* light winds to help keep what wind there is moving over the sail.

BEATING IN STRONG WINDS

Even with the easy-to-handle Topper this can be hard work, yet very rewarding. Sit out hard and aim for speed rather than close sailing to the wind — especially in waves which tend to stop the boat.

Setting the horse and mainsheet

The horse must be pulled as tight as possible so that when the mainsail is sheeted in hard (bending the mast and flattening the sail) the boom will not come too close to the centreline of the boat and cause excessive heeling forces and drag. Ease the sail to spill wind only when the boat heels beyond 15°.

Steering over waves

Try to steer so that the boat has an easy passage over the waves, luffing as you go up the wave and bearing away as you dip back down.

Daggerboard

When it is difficult to hold the boat upright, you will find it helps to raise the board to the first or even the second notch. This reduces heeling by allowing the boat to slip sideways.

Trim

Sit out as hard as possible keeping reasonably far forward — waves permitting. This reduces weather helm by tilting the sail's centre of effort forward of the daggerboard. Be ready to move aft quickly if the bow begins to bury itself.

Gusts

Watch for gusts approaching. Sit out and be prepared to spill wind from the sail.

Sail controls

The downhaul and outhaul need to be pulled quite tight. The kicking strap (vang) should be just tighter than if the slack is taken up after the mainsheet is pulled block to block. This is best achieved before the start of a race. It is also a satisfactory setting for off-wind work in strong winds.

BEATING — SOME COMMON MISTAKES

1 This boat is heeling too far; notice how much rudder has to be used to keep the boat going straight. The horse is also far too loose.

2 It is impossible to sail close to the wind unless the mainsheet is pulled in. Sitting farther forward will stop the stern (back) of the boat dragging through the water.

3 Here the wind is light and the boat would sail faster with a little more heel. Easing the outhaul would give more curve in the foot of the sail.

4 The foot of the sail is too loose this time!

10 Tacking

What is tacking?

The boat in Figure 1 is beating with the sail on the port side (a). The boat turns into the wind (b) and keeps turning until it is beating with the sail on the starboard side (c). This turn is called a tack.

Tacking in light to moderate winds

Never tack unless you are travelling at or near the maximum speed for the conditions. If the boat has insufficient momentum you will come to a stop and blow backwards ('get into irons') before you can point the boat onto the new tack. The following steps are demonstrated in the photo sequence below.

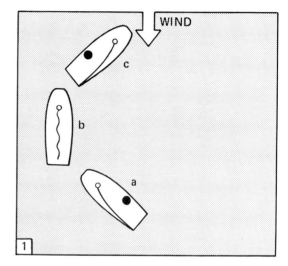

Tacking — step by step

1 Push the tiller gently but firmly away from you and at the same time sit out on the windward side.

2 Ease the mainsheet slightly and place it under the thumb of the hand that is holding the tiller extension. Let go with the other hand (see Figure 2).

3 As the boat begins to roll on top of you, start to move to the opposite side. Face the stern of the boat as you move, pushing the tiller extension in front of your body. As you reach the halfway point take the tiller extension in your 'new' steering hand and grasp the mainsheet in your 'new' sheet hand (Figure 3).

4 As the boat turns through the eye of the wind and begins to heel in the new direction, 'land' on the other deck.

5 Sit on the new side, steer straight ahead and pull in the mainsheet once again. Check that you are on a good close-hauled course by observing the luff of the sail (and wind indicator).

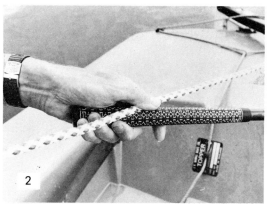

Tacking in strong winds

It is very easy to stall the boat in heavy weather. Here are some precautions to help avoid this.

- Always tack when travelling at maximum speed.

- Raise the daggerboard to the first or second notch to reduce weather helm.

- Do not push the tiller over too quickly. Roll the boat to windward just before you tack.

- As the sail comes over dive across the boat as quickly as possible, easing the mainsheet 2 feet.

- Sit out *hard* with your body weight well *forward* to counter the weather helm and sheet in again.

TACKING – SOME COMMON MISTAKES

1 Wait until the boat is head to wind before you cross to the 'new' side.

2 Face aft when you tack!

3 Don't turn too far. The burgee shows that I have swung round onto a *reach* after my tack.

Going faster

This is the one point of sailing where it is an advantage to be behind another boat, since you can blanket the boat in front of you and catch him up.

Here are some points to watch and ideas to try:

- Let the mainsheet out as far as possible.

- Make sure you have the daggerboard well up.

- Heel the boat to windward until the 'pull' on the tiller stops. You can now steer the boat by heel — if you heel it towards you the boat will turn away from you and vice versa.

- When a gust comes, run straight down wind with it. Try to stay with the gust as long as possible. If you see a gust to one side of the course, sail over to it and then ride it.

- Try to surf on waves as much as you can. Pull the mainsheet in a little as the boat accelerates down each wave (because the wind direction comes forward as you speed up).

RUNNING IN LIGHT WINDS

Trim

Sit well forward. Heel the boat to windward holding the boom right out with your hand. If the wind is so light that the sail falls out of shape it may be better to heel the boat to leeward, but watch the mainsheet doesn't drag in the water!

Steering

Use the tiller as little as possible.

Sail controls

All sail controls should be loose to encourage a full sail (see photo below).

RUNNING IN STRONG WINDS

Steering

Don't be in a hurry to get on a run when the wind is really blowing. Steer round gradually from a reach, letting the sail out slowly as you do so. Move back in the boat to help the bow lift.

If the boat starts to roll as you come onto the run, quickly pull the mainsheet a little. Keep a firm hand on the tiller, and don't let the boat turn back onto a reach.

Running by the lee (page 33) is a little risky for the unwary and can result in an unexpected gybe, but it can be a very effective way to avoid nosediving into a wave. The technique is to luff a little to catch a wave as it comes up behind you, then bear off quickly down the face of it. If, as you shoot down it, the bow looks as though it's going to bury itself in the wave ahead, sheet in and bear away further. The act of bearing off just

before an imminent nosedive reduces the pressure in the sail (as does sheeting in) and greatly reduces the tendency for the bow to go under. But do watch the accidental gybe!

Adjusting the sail

Although you may lose a little speed, it is often safest to tie a knot in your mainsheet to prevent the boom from going out square.

Rolling is caused particularly by the top of the sail twisting forward in a gust and pushing the boat over to windward. Keep the daggerboard at least half down to dampen rolling.

Sail controls

If it is really blowing it is not worth easing the sail controls — you won't gain much and time will be lost resetting on the next leg of the course.

RUNNING — SOME COMMON MISTAKES

1 The downhaul is far too tight. Note the creases in the sail along the mast.

2 The kicking strap in this picture is much too loose — the sail is losing drive and may force the boat to heel to windward.

3 Don't let the mainsheet out too far! .

4 Sit back in strong winds! Sheet in quickly if the boat begins to nosedive.

12 Gybing

What is gybing?

In Figure 1, boat (a) is running with the sail on the starboard side. The helmsman turns through a small angle (b) and the wind forces the sail out to the port side of the boat (c). This turn is called a *gybe*.

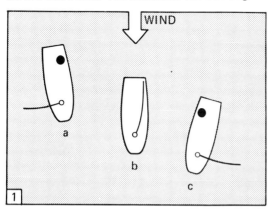

Why is gybing difficult?

Gybing is the hardest sailing manoeuvre. Unlike tacking, the wind pushes on the sail throughout the turn. The boat is moving at high speed, so is very sensitive to tiller movements. A miscalculation results in the boat rolling — with the sail 'edge on' there's not much to dampen the roll and the helmsman tends to take an involuntary dip.

Decide when you want to gybe, and then do it! The best moment is when the boat is moving fast down a wave — since you're travelling away from the wind, the 'push' on the sail is lessened.

Six steps to a good gybe

1 *Get ready*. Push the daggerboard half down (never gybe with the board right up or right down). Bear away until the wind is almost directly behind the boat. (See photo sequence below.)

2 *Pull in the mainsheet.* Pull in an arm's length of mainsheet, face aft, and heel the boat to windward (if you let it heel away from you, you can't turn).

3 *Change hands.* Clamp the mainsheet under the thumb of the hand holding the tiller extension. Let go with the other hand.

4 *Turn.* Bear away further until the boom comes across (don't forget to duck!). At the same time grip the leeward gunwale with your free hand.

5 *Cross the boat.* As the boom comes over cross the boat facing aft. Reach under the mainsheet and grasp the tiller extension with your free hand. Lift the mainsheet with your other hand, giving a short pull to prevent the sheet fouling up in the rudder stock.

6 *Straighten up.* 'Reverse' the tiller hard to bring the boat back on course.

Gybing in strong winds

When the wind is very strong it is safer (though slower) to gybe without pulling in any mainsheet before the gybe. You will need to bear away a lot further before the sail comes over but when it does it will just fly harmlessly out on the other side like a flag. As you bear away again onto the new run be careful that the boat doesn't roll on top of you!

If you consider that a capsize is almost inevitable you may prefer to wear round. This involves turning through almost 360° as shown in Figure 2. Do this with the daggerboard half up; pull in the mainsheet and spin the boat around fast.

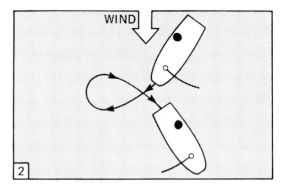

GYBING — SOME COMMON MISTAKES

1 It is useless to go into a gybe heeling to leeward. The heeled boat tries to turn the wrong way.

2 If the daggerboard is too far up the boom will catch it as you gybe, with interesting results.

3 Straighten up after your gybe or you could broach (swing right round into the wind, capsizing as you go!).

13 Capsizing

Everyone capsizes. Indeed, if you don't capsize sometimes, you're probably not really trying.

When the inevitable happens, try to stay on top of the boat. In most other classes, the crew needs to swim to right the boat. In the Topper this is unnecessary.

Never leave the boat (to swim for the shore, for example). The hull will support you almost indefinitely — it has reserve buoyancy inside and will float even if the skin is punctured — and is more easily spotted than a swimmer.

The boat will tip one of two ways: to leeward (which is more pleasant) or to windward.

Capsizing to leeward

Try to turn round as the boat capsizes so you are facing 'uphill'. Climb over the side and on to the daggerboard, then lean back and slowly pull the boat upright. If you do this slowly, the boat automatically turns into the wind. At the last moment, straddle the deck and scramble into the cockpit.

Even if the boat turns upside down, this is no problem in a Topper (see photo sequence). Climb on the hull, stand with your back to the wind and lever the boat onto its side. Try to stay on the daggerboard; you can then right the boat as described on the previous page.

If you do fall off the daggerboard, try pulling down on it while you are in the water. If this fails, swim round and use the mast as a step to get yourself on top of the boat. Then begin again!

Avoiding a capsize to leeward

- Watch for gusts.

- Keep the mainsheet in your hand at all times.

- Sit out hard in strong winds.

- On a reach or run, avoid letting the boat turn into the wind.

Capsizing to windward

Try to stay on top of the boat. However, you may well fall out as the boat capsizes to windward. If this happens on a reach or run, hang on to the mainsheet at all costs – the boat is travelling fast and may finish up some distance away. The mainsheet is your lifeline. Do *not* hang on to the tiller extension which may snap as you go over the side.

1 Pull yourself back to the boat along the mainsheet. Climb *over the boat* onto the daggerboard.

2 Gently lever the mast out of the water. As the wind picks it up, straddle the side deck. As the boat begins to come upright, get your body into the cockpit and across to the windward side. You need to move very fast to prevent the boat capsizing again to leeward.

3 If the boat does capsize again, go over the side
   onto the daggerboard once more, and right
   the boat as for a capsize to leeward.

In shallow water, don't let the boat turn upside
down or the mast may snap.
   If the mast gets stuck in mud, stand on the
daggerboard close to the hull and gently bounce
up and down to free it.

Avoiding a capsize to windward

- Be ready to move your weight inboard in lulls.

- Pull in the mainsheet rapidly if the boat rolls
  to windward.

- On a reach or run, avoid turning fast away
  from the wind.

14 Landing

Think ahead before landing since a great deal of damage can result if care is not taken. Always try to land on a windward shore if you can because this makes it easier to stop!

Landing on a windward shore

1 Sail slowly towards the shore. Control the boat's speed by letting out the mainsheet. Ease the horse so the tiller can be raised to pull up the rudder later.

2 At the last minute, turn into the wind and quickly lift out the daggerboard (Figure 1) and raise the rudder (Figure 2).

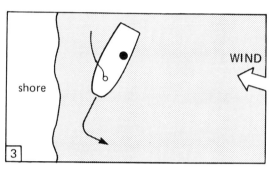

close to the shore as the depth of water will allow before luffing head to wind, jumping out (Figure 4) and holding the boat by the bow. Ask someone on shore to bring you your launching trolley.

In surf, this technique does not work! Simply pull up the rudder and daggerboard and sail fast through the surf, straight towards the beach. Keep going straight until the bow grounds, jump out and then drag the boat up the beach before the next wave arrives.

3 Step into the water on the shore side of the boat, holding it as near the bow as you can.

Landing on a lee shore

There may be times when landing on a lee shore is unavoidable. In this case approach the shore on whichever reach is closest to the wind direction (Figure 3). Raise the daggerboard and rudder as far as possible while still keeping control. Let the sail out so that it is half flapping and not causing the boat to heel or go particularly fast. Sail in as

15 Going faster

More than half the Toppers produced will never be raced — so the gear provided with the standard boat is kept fairly basic so that the boat can be sold at a very competitive price. The Topper International Class Association recognizes the limitations of the standard boat, however, and has drafted the class rules to allow certain alterations to the basic gear. I have designed a race pack which greatly improves sail control and should be considered by every keen Topper helm. It is available as an accessory or, more economically, as an alternative to the standard rope set if purchased with a new Topper.

Downhaul (Cunningham)

It is desirable to tighten the luff (front edge) of the sail as the wind increases by tensioning the downhaul. The class rules allow a 3:1 system and the arrangement shown in Figure 1 benefits from the maximum allowable purchase whilst also giving a direct pull towards one's body.

Outhaul

Because the position of the outhaul cleat on the boom is fixed, the pull on the outhaul is away from one's body and hence it is desirable to take advantage of the maximum allowable 4:1 purchase. With the system shown in Figure 2 it is possible to tension the foot when beating in a force 5 wind (although it will be easier if you tension the foot before rounding the leeward mark!).

To avoid having a very long rope (the rules require it to be possible to take two rolls of mainsail around the mast), one end of the multi-purchase system is hooked to this kicking strap take-off eye. When reefing this hook is detached, making the system 1:1.

The standard clew tie-down is replaced with a metal ring/hook (Figure 3); this slides along the boom better than the rope version, is easier to attach and holds the clew (corner of the sail) close to the boom.

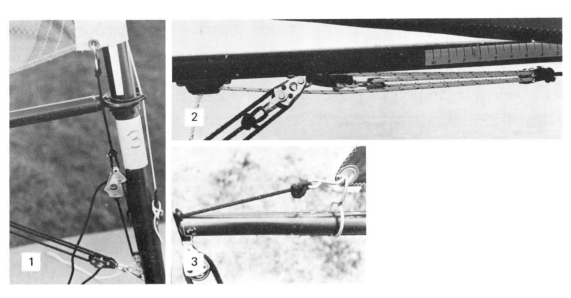

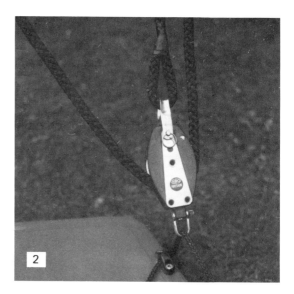

Kicking strap (vang)

The 3:1 system shown in Figure 1 makes it possible to adjust the kicking strap tension while sailing, particularly if a swivel is fitted between the jamb cleat and mast. This way the pull can be angled directly towards your body. Please note that if this system is inverted with the loose end of line coming from the boom it would then be an illegal 4:1 system.

Mainsheet

The bottom block on the mainsheet can be replaced with a ratchet block which allows the sheet to be pulled in easily but holds the rope when the sheet tension is eased slightly. This reduces the load on the mainsheet considerably, making it much less tiring for young helms to hold the sheet in tight for long beats. These ratchet blocks usually have the ability to be switched off for light winds or downwind work. More sophisticated ones shown in Figure 2 automatically release the ratchet when the load is much reduced (e.g. when reaching).

Halyard

Replacement of the halyard by a prestretched one will hold the sail right up to the top of the mast; this allows maximum bend to be achieved on the mast before the mainsheet blocks come together.

Daggerboard

Apart from the sail controls, one other important modification is to the daggerboard friction device. (New Toppers now have this modification.)

On the original standard boat two hands were needed to move the daggerboard up or down. If you have this type then advantage can be gained by removing the retaining elastic and arranging another piece of elastic line to pull the board towards the mast (Figure 3). The elastic must be pulled round the mast and clipped back onto itself to conform with the Class rules. This system enables you to move the board up or down with one hand, while the elastic pulls the

board forward giving enough friction to hold it in any position.

Sitting out (hiking) technique

When you are racing in strong winds your speed, particularly to windward, will be directly related to your ability to hold the boat upright and this means sitting out! The further out you can get, the greater leverage you can exert to counter the heeling moment of the sail. Whilst the shallow depth of the Topper precludes a classical sitting-out position with knees bent, it is remarkable how soon you will become accustomed to sitting out straight-legged.

The use of the centre toestrap is absolutely essential, even if you are over 6ft tall. It enables you to sit out a lot further. If your boat does not have a centre toestrap then buy the conversion kit and fit it! If you haven't trained yourself to use it then do so — even on the reaches — you will go much faster in a blow.

Precise sheeting

It is impossible to be certain that you have set the mainsheet perfectly. Watch the boats around you — if they are going faster and you reckon that you are sailing well, try altering the tension on the mainsheet and thereby the exact shape of the sail — trial and error is essential for that last tenth of a knot!

You may find the following tables useful in setting up your boat for various conditions.

Adjustments for beating

Light winds and smooth water		
	Action	*Reasons*
Trim	Heel boat until leeward gunwale nearly under water.	Gravity will help keep the sail full. Skin friction is reduced to a minimum.
Mainsheet	Ease slightly, i.e. blocks about 5 inches apart.	To give a little fullness and a slight twist in the sail.
Horse	Ease off approx. 1 inch from bar tight.	To compensate for the mainsheet being eased the bottom block needs to be allowed to come nearer the centre line and thus bring the boom inboard.
Outhaul	Ease to give 4 inches of draft at centre of foot.	To give increased drive (heeling forces are not a consideration in these conditions).
Downhaul	Minimum tension only.	To prevent fullness being pulled forward in the sail, as this will impair pointing ability.
Kicking strap (vang)	Tensioned just to take up slack when mainsheet is tensioned as above.	This tension will give correct twist when reaching and running. It will have no effect on sail shape when beating.
Daggerboard	Fully down.	For maximum pointing and minimum leeway.

Moderate winds and smooth water

	Action	Reasons
Trim	Heel boat about 10°.	To reduce wetted area.
Mainsheet	Very tight — block to block (note: main halyard needs to be very tight to prevent sail slipping down the mast).	To bend mast and flatten sail for maximum pointing ability. With good steering conditions the twist-free sail that this gives is also desirable.
Horse	Tight.	To position boom just over the stern quarter.
Outhaul	Slightly tighter than for light conditions — say 3 inches of draft at midpoint of foot.	Still no excessive side forces, yet more than for light winds.
Downhaul	Only very slightly tighter than for light weather.	To just remove the added creases due to the fully bent mast, without pulling the fullness too far forward.
Kicking strap (vang)	Just take up the slack after mainsheet is tensioned.	Not effective on beat but will give a relatively twist-free sail on reach and run.
Daggerboard	Fully down.	Maximum pointing and minimum leeway.

Moderate winds and choppy sea

	Action	Reasons
Trim	Heel a little less than 10°.	Wetted area difficult to reduce in waves. Less water finds its way into the cockpit if you heel a little less than normal.
Mainsheet	Ease mainsheet to give about 3-4 inches between the blocks.	This gives a little fullness in the sail to punch through the waves and a little twist in the sail to counter the erratic steering conditions.
Horse	Tight.	To keep boom off the centre line — drive is more important than pointing.
Outhaul	About 4 inches of draft as for light winds, unless heeling forces demand maximum sitting out when the outhaul will need tightening.	Unless overpowered, maximum drive is desirable.
Downhaul	Slight tension only.	Keep fullness aft in sail for maximum drive.
Kicking strap (vang)	Take up slack when mainsheet is correctly sheeted.	Not effective on the beat but will give the correct twist on the reach and run.
Daggerboard	Fully down.	Gives minimum leeway.

Strong winds and moderate waves		
	Action	*Reasons*
Trim	Try to keep the boat as upright as possible.	It is easier to hold the boat upright than to get it back upright after it heels.
Mainsheet	Try to keep mainsheet tight but spill wind rather than heel excessively.	Easing the sheet puts fullness in the sail and therefore should only be done as a last resort.
Horse	Exceedingly tight.	To try to hold the boom down (bending mast) while letting it out as far as possible (reducing side forces).
Outhaul	Tight. Foot of sail just beginning to curl up.	To reduce draft in sail and hence side (heeling) forces.
Downhaul	Tight.	To pull fullness forward and reduce side forces in the middle and upper parts of the sail.
Kicking strap (vang)	Tight.	Push down on the boom (so it is lower than mainsheet block-to-block) and tighten the kicking strap so the mast is bent even when the sheet is eased in a squall.
Daggerboard	Raise slightly if overpowered.	To reduce heeling moment and move centre of lateral resistance aft — thus reducing weather helm.

'Feeling' the boat when sailing to windward

With practice you will find that in most wind conditions you will be able to sail to windward without looking to see if the sail is lifting. You will also learn to be very sensitive about the amount the boat is heeling; if you luff too close to the wind the normal heel will decrease, returning again as you bear away. It is quite easy to sail a Topper extremely fast to windward simply by watching the angle of the horizon and listening to the noise of the water on the hull: when you sail too close to the wind the speed falls off and you *hear* the boat slowing down. Be aware — use all your senses — and become a faster sailor.

Physical fitness

Although the Topper is not a demanding boat physically, it is essential to be agile and fit to get the best out of your boat. If you cannot sail two or three times a week, then keep fit in other ways — remember if you feel physically fit you'll be mentally fit as well!

16 Racing

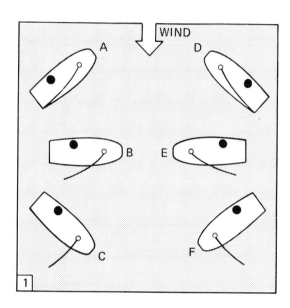

THE RULES

A full discussion of the rules is outside the scope of this book. For the cautious beginner, a few key rules will keep him out of trouble in most cases.

Boats meeting on opposite tacks

A boat is either on a port tack or a starboard tack. It is on a port tack if the wind is blowing over its port side. In Figure 1, boats A, B and C are on port tack; boats D, E and F are on starboard tack.

A port tack boat must keep clear of a starboard tack boat.

D, E and F have right of way over A, B and C, who must keep clear.

Boats meeting on the same tack

If the boats are overlapped (i.e. if the bow of the following boat is ahead of a line at right angles to the stern of the leading boat) the following rule applies:

A windward boat shall keep clear of a leeward boat.

In Figure 2, G must keep clear of H, I must keep clear of J and L must keep clear of K.

If the boats are *not* overlapped (Figure 3):

A boat clear astern shall keep clear of a boat clear ahead.

M is overtaking and is not allowed to sail into the back of N.

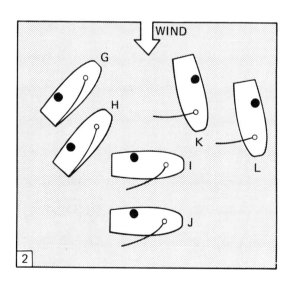

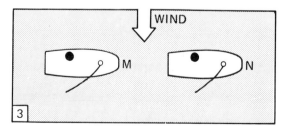

50

Mark Laity

Boats meeting at marks

An outside boat shall give each boat overlapping it on the inside room to round or pass the mark.

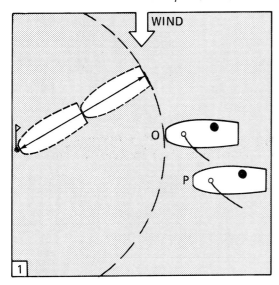

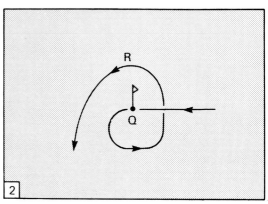

O must give P room to go round the mark on the inside. P must get his overlap on O before O's bow reaches an imaginary circle of radius two boat's lengths from the mark (Fig. 1). In the photo, the boats are rounding the buoy to starboard (clockwise). The boat nearest the camera has the right to turn inside the other boat.

Note that this rule does not apply at starts (see page 53).

Penalties

If you hit a mark, you must go round it again. You have no rights while you are re-rounding (from point Q to point R) (Figure 2).

If you hit another boat and reckon you're in the right, protest by flying a red flag (a small piece of cloth clothespegged to your kicking strap (vang) is the simplest method). Argue your case in the protest room afterwards.

If you hit another boat and are in the wrong, you must either retire or, if the rules allow (they usually do), make a 720° turn. In effect, you have to tack, gybe, tack again and gybe again — then sail on (Figure 3).

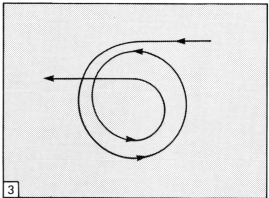

THE LINE START

The start is the most important part of the race. If you get a bad start, you have to overtake every-one to win — while you're battling past the oppo-sition, the leaders are sailing further ahead. If you get a good start, you're sailing in clear air.

How is a race started?

Most races are started on a beat. The race com-mittee sets an (imaginary) start line, usually between the mast of the committee boat (A) and a buoy (B) (Figure 4). They often lay another buoy (C), which does not have to be on the line. Boats are not allowed to sail between C and A.

Ten minutes before the start the class flag (or a white shape) is raised on the committee boat and a gun is fired.

Five minutes before the start the blue peter (or a blue shape) is raised and a gun is fired.

At the start, both flags are lowered (or a red shape is raised) and a gun is fired.

Boats must be behind the start line when the starting gun is fired. Your aim is to be just behind the line, sailing at full speed, when the gun fires.

How can I get a good start?

Set your watch at the ten-minute gun, and check it at the five-minute gun.

During the last few minutes, avoid the 'danger' areas X and Y. From X you cannot get on to the start line because the boats to leeward have right of way. Boat D, for example, will be forced the wrong side of buoy C. In Y you are bound to pass the wrong side of buoy B. Boat F has this problem.

Don't go too far from the line — 30 yards is plenty. A wall of boats builds up on the line in the last two minutes, and you must be in that wall. If you're behind it, not only can you not get in, but your wind is cut off by the wall.

Aim to be six boat lengths behind the line with 45 seconds to go — closer if boats to windward are moving ahead of you. Control your speed with careful use of the mainsheet. Keep the boat moving forward slowly — most of the sail will be flapping but take care not to stop or you will have no steerage way. With ten seconds to go you should be two lengths behind the line. Pull in the mainsheet, sit out and start beating. You should cross the line just after the gun with full speed. Boat G has followed this advice.

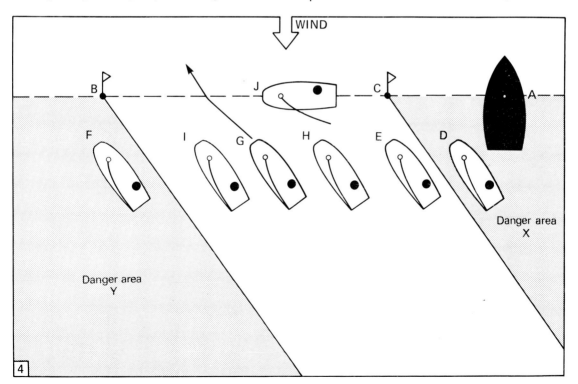

What about the other boats?

It's important to watch out for other boats as you line up to start. G has right of way over H, but must keep clear of I. As you line up, keep turning into the wind a little. This keeps you away from the boat to leeward — it also opens up a nice 'hole' to leeward that you can sail down into at the start (for extra speed).

Don't reach down the line with 15 seconds to go like boat J. You will have no rights over G, H and I who will sail into you. If you're too early, let the sail out in good time and slow down.

Which end of the line should I start?

So far, the wind has been at right angles to the start line. As far as the wind is concerned it will not matter where on the line you start.

Usually, however, the wind is not at right angles to the line. You can find out what it's doing by sailing down the line on a reach. Adjust the sail so the front just flaps (Figure 1).

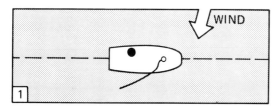

Keeping the mainsheet in the same position, tack and reach back down the line. In Figure 2,

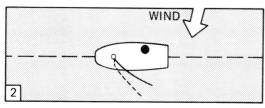

the sail will now be too far in — you will have to let the mainsheet out to make it flap. This indicates the wind is blowing from the starboard end of the line — and you should start at this end.

How do I make a starboard end start?

Sail slowly, and as close to the wind as possible, so you will reach the windward end of the line with the gun (Figure 3). Boats to windward have no rights and are forced out. Boats to lee-

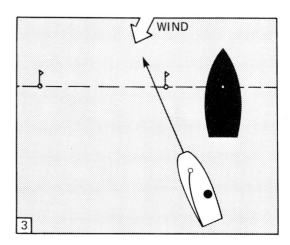

ward can't touch you — you are already sailing as close to the wind as possible.

How do I make a port end start?

Keep near the port end of the line (Figure 4). Aim to cross as near the buoy as possible. Tack on to port tack as soon as you can clear the fleet.

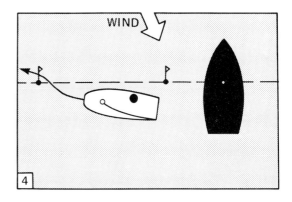

THE GATE START

A gate start is made by crossing the wake of a boat called the pathfinder which is beating on port tack in front of the fleet. In theory everyone has an equally good start, because the earlier you start the further you have to sail.

The pathfinder, who is selected by the race committee from among the competitors, waits near the committee boat while the usual sound and flag signals are made. About one minute before the start the pathfinder sets off on port tack, accompanied by two motor boats, the gate

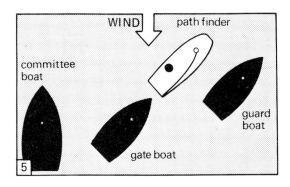

boat and guard boat, to protect it from overenthus-
iastic competitors. (See Figure 5.) A few
seconds before the start a free-floating buoy is
dropped over the back of the gate boat to mark
the port (left-hand) end of the line. After the
start competitors (on starboard tack) pass closely
behind the gate boat (Figure 6). The line gradually lengthens, and the boats start one at a time.
A late start is no disadvantage, since the pathfinder is sailing up the beat for you while you're
waiting.

How can I get a good start?

You need to know the course the pathfinder will
take. So, with about four minutes to go, begin
beating on port tack from the committee boat.
After two or three minutes bear away onto a
reach, then tack and wait with your sail flapping

(like boat Y in Figure 6). Watch for the pathfinder, and control your speed so that you beat
slowly up to the stern of the guard boat. As you
go behind it, pick up speed by bearing away
slightly and sitting out. Then beat, flat out, to
pass just behind the stern of the gate boat.

NEVER reach towards the guard boat like
boat X. You have no rights over boats D and E
who will push you into the guard boat or gate
boat. If you hit either, you will be disqualified.
If you find yourself in boat X's position, try to
tack onto port and bear away. When you're
ready, tack back onto starboard and try again.
If all else fails, point into the wind and stop!

How can I recover from a bad start?

If you start too far from the gate boat, your only
option is to sail through the gate, then tack onto
port and sail behind the whole fleet to the right-
hand side of the course. If that turns out to be
the best side, you could find yourself ahead at
the windward mark!

Where should I start?

Start late if you think you are slower than the
pathfinder, if you think the pathfinder will hit a
permanent header (see page 57) or if the tide is
more favourable to the right of the course.
Otherwise start early.

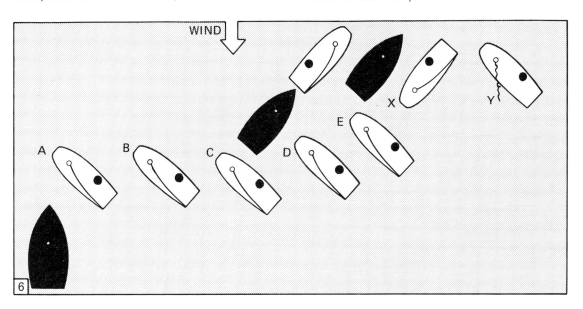

THE BEAT

After the tension of the start, it's important to settle down and concentrate on sailing hard.

What about other boats?

A boat when beating casts a 'wind shadow' — shown in Figure 1. It also creates an area of disturbed air to windward due to the wind being deflected by the sail; the air behind the boat is also disturbed.

You should therefore avoid sailing just to windward of another boat, behind it or in its wind shadow. In the diagram, boat B should either tack or bear away to clear its wind. Boats D and F should both tack.

Which way should I go?

You may have to modify your course to take account of tides and windshifts, but your first aim should be to make reasonably long tacks to start with, shortening them as you approach the windward mark.

Don't sail into the area indicated by the shaded part of Figure 2 — if you do, you will have to reach in to the buoy and will lose valuable time and distance. Stay inside the lay lines — these are the paths you would sail when beating to hit the windward mark.

When approaching the windward mark on the first beat in a big fleet it is advisable not to arrive at the mark on port tack. For safety's sake make your final approach on starboard tack.

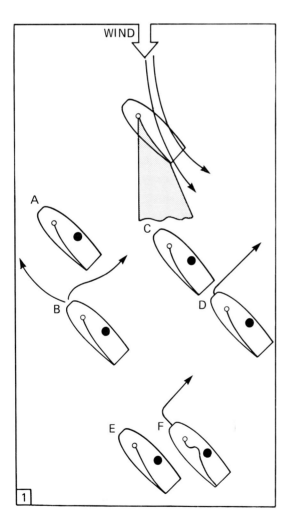

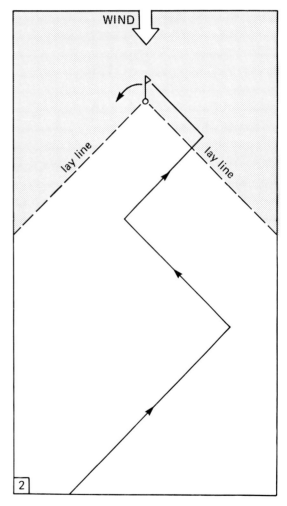

Windshifts

Once you are confident at beating and can tack efficiently, you are ready to start using windshifts.

The wind constantly alters in direction about its mean. Some of the shifts are more pronounced and last longer than others — it is these that you have to spot and use.

In shifty winds, stay close to the middle of the beat. Tack each time the wind heads you (forces you to alter course *away* from the mark). In Figure 3, the boat takes no account of windshifts. Note how little progress it makes compared with the boat in Figure 4, which tacks each time the wind heads it.

The main problem is to differentiate between a real shift and a short-lived change in the wind. For that reason, sail on into each shift for five or ten seconds to make sure it's going to last. If a header lasts that long, tack.

If you find yourself tacking too often, or are confused, sail on one tack for a while until you're sure what the wind is doing. Remember that you lose at least a boat's length each time you tack, so there has to be a good reason to do so.

How can I get up the beat faster?

- Keep your wind clear.

- Watch for windshifts.

- Keep near the middle of the course.

- Practise tacking.

- Get fit — then you can sit out harder.

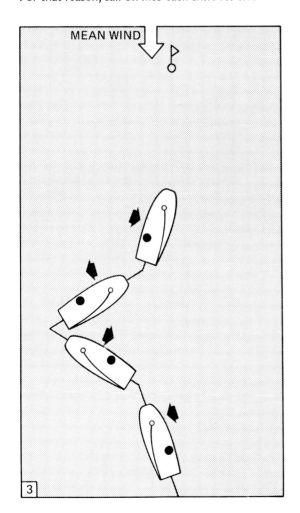

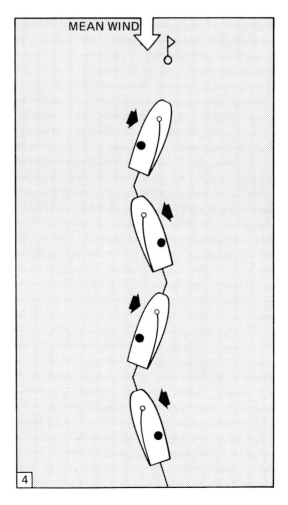

THE REACH

If it's blowing hard, pull the daggerboard half up before you bear away round the windward mark. Turn slowly, moving your weight back and letting out the mainsheet.

What course should I steer?

The quickest way down the reach is a straight line from one mark to the next. However, if your rivals let you sail this course, you're lucky! The problem is that overtaking boats (e.g. A in Figure 1) push up to windward. The boats to leeward (e.g. B) get nervous about their wind being stolen and steer high also. The result is that everyone sails an enormous arc (X), losing ground on the leaders.

You have to decide whether or not to go on the 'great circle'; the alternative is to sail a leeward path (Y). You have to go down far enough to avoid the blanketing effect of the boats to windward — but usually you will sail a shorter distance than they do. You will also get the inside turn at the gybe mark. You can go for the leeward route on the second reach too, but this time you will be on the outside at the turn.

How can I get down the reach faster?

- Follow the tips for fast reaching on page 20, 'Going faster'.

- Keep your wind clear.

- Sail the shortest route.

- Go for the inside turn at marks.

Starting the next beat

As you approach the leeward mark, tighten the downhaul and push down the daggerboard. Steer round the mark so that you leave it very close (like boat C). Don't come in to the mark close (like boat D) or you'll start the beat well to leeward of your rivals.

Sit out, and go!

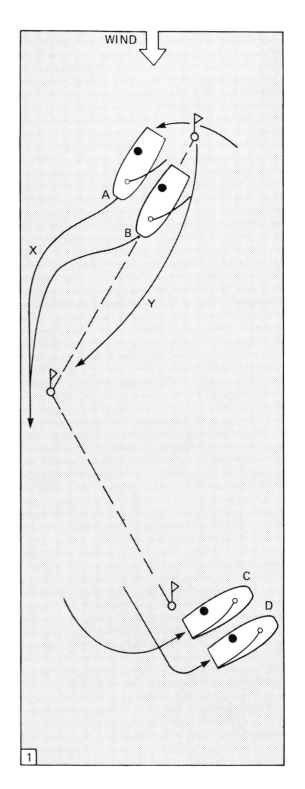

THE RUN

In strong winds, take your time as you bear away on to a run. Pull the daggerboard half up, sit back and adjust the mainsheet as you turn. If the boat starts to roll, steer a straight course and pull in the mainsheet a little. Continue to bear away when the boat is under control.

What course should I steer?

The quickest route is a straight line to the leeward mark (Figure 1).

In very strong winds, you may not be able to control the boat on a straight downwind run. An alternative is to follow course Z, wearing round (see page 39) rather than gybing at the midpoint.

The presence of other boats may also prevent your steering a straight course. Boat F is blanketed by boat E — it can escape by steering to one side (course M or N). Other things being equal, N would be better since it gives the inside turn at the next mark.

Boat E is correct to blanket F in this way. E can attack from a range of up to four boat's lengths; it can sail right up behind F, turning to one side at the last moment to overtake. E must, of course, keep clear of F during this manoeuvre.

Watch out for boats still beating, especially when running on port tack. Alter course in good time to avoid them — a last-minute turn could capsize you.

What about crowding at the leeward mark?

It often happens that several boats arrive at the leeward mark together. The inside berth is the place to aim for — H, I and J have to give G room to turn inside them. If you're in J's position, it's better to slow down and wait to turn close to the buoy rather than sail round the outside of the pack. Try to anticipate this situation, and slow down and move across to the inside in good time. Try to get G's position.

As you get near the leeward mark, tighten the downhaul and push the daggerboard down. Turn slowly and aim to leave the mark close (course P). You will need to pull in a good length of mainsheet as you round the mark — pull it in with your front hand and clamp it under a finger of your tiller hand while you change grip for the next pull.

How can I get down the run faster?

- Follow the 'Going faster' tips on p. 35.
- Keep your wind clear.
- Sail the shortest route.
- Go for the inside turn at the leeward mark.

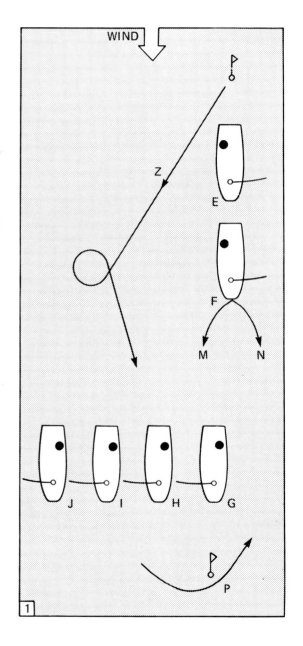

CURRENTS AND TIDES

When sailing, you must take account of currents and tides. Naturally, when sailing against the current you will look for a course where the current is weakest, and when you are sailing with the current you will go where it is strongest. The current is weakest in shallow water and near the shore (where friction with the land slows it down).

Before you go afloat make sure you know the likely strength and direction of the tides across the race course.

Beating against the tide

Enormous gains can be made at the start over the majority of the competition who will disregard the effect of the tide. Get to the line early and stem the tide with the sail flapping — it is often possible to have a whole boat's length lead over boats around you in these circumstances.

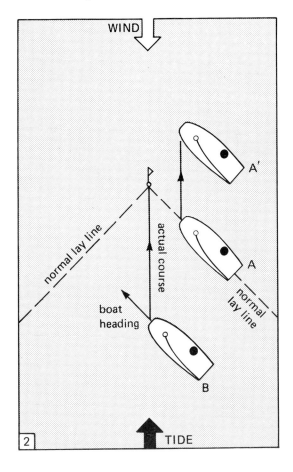

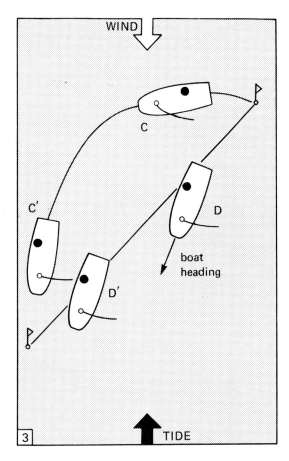

Beating with the tide

Starting is difficult since in these circumstances the majority of the fleet will be early resulting in many general recalls. You have no alternative but to keep in line with the front rank of starters.

Great gains can be made however on the beat and reach in wind-against-tide conditions. Figure 2 shows how easy it is to overstand the windward mark if you go to the normal lay line; boat A expected just to lay the mark but is swept well upwind; boat B gets it right. You can gain many places by keeping near the middle of the course, always tacking well within the lay lines.

On the reach, helms unaware of the effect of the tide will sail a considerably greater distance (Figure 3). They may end up running into the tide like boat C — this is very slow! Boat D allows for the tidal effect and sails straight to the mark.

61

17 Care and maintenance

STORAGE

With a hull depth of only 15 inches, the Topper is very easy to store and takes up a very small space. If you are storing out of doors it is perfectly satisfactory to stand the boat on its gunwale against a wall; you can pull it tight against the wall by passing a rope out through the daggerboard case and tightening this on to a piece of timber set at right angles to the slot. If you have room to keep the boat flat, raise it off the ground a few inches to allow air to circulate. (The photographs show the best support points.) There is no need to cover the boat — foul weather will have no detrimental effect at all on the polypropylene hull.

If you have the use of a garage, there is usually enough height to sling a Topper from the roof above the car. You can use the roof rack straps as slings and these should pass around the hull — forward beneath the mast step position and aft below the rear bulkhead. The easiest method of lifting the boat into the required position is to drive it in, right way up on the car roof. This way you have the minimum of lifting to contend with!

ROUTINE MAINTENANCE

Hull

The material from which Topper hulls are moulded is extremely tough and is the same all the way through. So you are not concerned — as with a GRP hull — about damaging the gel-coat and allowing water to penetrate. However, polypropylene is a little softer than GRP and *is* inclined to scratch with harsh treatment. With sensible use and reasonable care, it is quite feasible to keep the bottom in good shape; minor scuffs and scratches can be removed with fine wet-and-dry paper, and a reasonable shine restored with a good cutting compound. More severe scratches are best tackled with a sharp cabinet scraper or even a very sharp, *very* finely set smoothing plane. The material cuts beautifully but does not respond well to coarse sanding, which can leave a furry surface which will do nothing for your boat speed. Major shunts — usually the result of a boat becoming detached from its roof rack — can result in a split hull. This can be satisfactorily repaired by a special hot-air welding process and the manufacturers will advise on your nearest specialist.

Spars

These should rarely require any maintenance although it is a good idea to check the riveted eyes for security — particularly if you are going out in heavy weather. Rivets have been known to break and for peace of mind it is a good idea to replace them with large self-tapping stainless steel screws. Always use the fattest ones that will go through the fitting. Cleats can also break or 'burn out', but make sure you check the class rules thoroughly to ensure that you do not replace them with anything that could put you out of class.

Rudder and daggerboard

These are injection moulded in polypropylene, and glass-reinforced to give them the required stiffness and hard surface. No maintenance at all is required apart from keeping the tips smooth and free of indentations by the judicious use of wet-and-dry paper. Always check the rudder bolts for correct tightness — there should be no slop between the blade and the cast aluminium stock, nor should it be so tight so as to prevent

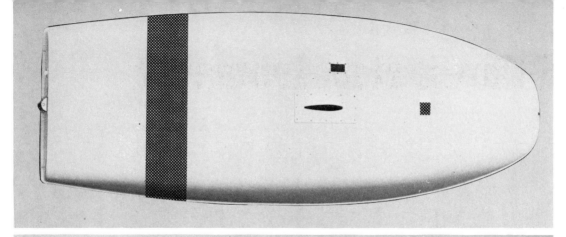

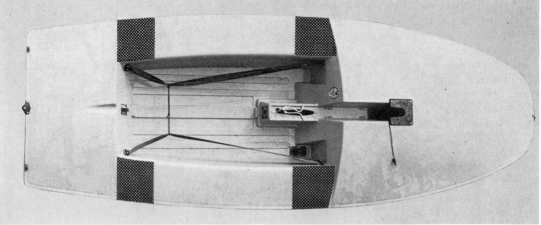

the blade from retracting properly. Tiller extensions have been known to detach themselves at the least convenient moments so it is worth checking frequently that the connecting bolt is secure and properly locked. The latest Toppers have a riveted connection here, but if your boat is of the older type, it is sensible to 'rivet' over the end of the bolt.

Sail

This is the 'engine' of your Topper and if you race the boat it is absolutely essential to keep it in peak 'tune'. There is no doubt that all sails have a life-span, so according to how often you use your Topper you will have to replace the sail from time to time. Nevertheless, sensible treatment and care can extend this life-span considerably. Never crumple a sail into its bag after use — always fold it carefully, concertina fashion across the sail parallel to the boom, finally rolling it up as loosely as possible. An even better system is to roll the sail around a spar, which is slightly

less convenient to transport but does totally eliminate creasing. Creasing will not ruin the sail, but could make it that little bit less efficient.

Salt water will have no short-term ill effects but always rinse the sail thoroughly in fresh water prior to storage.

Fastenings

There are a number of machine screws on the Topper's hull and these are threaded into expanding brass inserts which work in a similar fashion to a rawlplug. They should be checked periodically for tightness but be careful not to overtighten.

Self bailer and mast gate

These do not require lubrication but it helps to keep them operating efficiently if you rinse them frequently with fresh water to clear away any abrasive sand and grit that could shorten their lives.

18 The Topper Club

The Topper is one of the world's fastest-growing dinghy classes and enjoys one of the best-supported and administered class associations.

The Topper International Class Association (TICA) has divisions in many countries. Most buyers of new Toppers automatically receive one year's free membership of TICA and membership is mandatory to be eligible for TICA events.

There are many benefits of belonging to TICA: members receive free of charge the quarterly magazine *Topper Times* which gives full information and reports on Topper events, regattas and other social activities. The association defines (and polices) the rules of the class — making sure that racing is fair and that older boats remain competitive. And, perhaps most important of all, the association will help you communicate with other Topper sailors and thus enjoy your boat to the full — whether you are a beginner or a budding world champion!

The addresses of your National and International Secretaries can be obtained from the manufacturers:

Topper International Limited
Kingsnorth Technology Park
Wotton Road
Ashford, Kent TN23 2LN
England